WITHDRAWN FROM STOCK

Tell me about...

Martial Arts

Published in 2009 by Evans Publishing Ltd,
2A Portman Mansions,
Chiltern St, London WIU 6NR

© Evans Brothers Limited 2009

Editor: Nicola Edwards
Designer: D.R. Ink
All photographs by Wishlist except for page 6   Jung Yeon-Je/AFP/Getty Images; page 8 Kazuhiro
Nogi/AFP/Getty Images; page 14 Sam Yeh/AFP/Getty Images; page 15 Shaun Botterill/Getty Images; page
18 Paul Gilham/Getty Images for DAGOC; page 21 Jung Yeon-Je/AFP/Getty Images; page 22 Alexander
Blotnitsky/AFP/Getty Images; page 26 Vladimir Rys/Bongarts/Getty Images; page 27 Toshifumi
Kitamura/AFP/Getty Images

British Library Cataloguing in Publication Data

Gifford, Clive
   Martial arts. - (Tell me about sport)
   1. Martial arts - Juvenile literature
   I. Title
   796.8

ISBN-13: 9780237536336

Printed in China.

Printed on chlorine free paper from sustainable sources.

Contents

Martial arts

▲

Top martial artists test themselves out in competitions and tournaments. Here, a referee watches a contest at the 2008 Tae kwon do Invitational Tournament in China.

The word martial means "to do with war" and martial arts are ways of fighting and training to fight. Some of the first martial arts were designed to kill or harm opponents. Others were invented to help people defend themselves from attack. This is called self-defence.

Most of the martial arts began in Asia. During the 20th century, many martial arts teachers left Asia and began teaching in America and Europe. Today, millions of people all over the world take part in martial arts. They enjoy challenging themselves with different moves, in training and in competition.

Limerick County Library

Every martial art has its own style and rules. Some martial arts such as karate and kickboxing are split into many different styles. These are called schools or systems. The martial art of kung fu has more than 400 different schools.

One of the great things about most martial arts is that you can start learning them at any age. There are classes for children from nursery age to teenagers.

Once you get into a martial art, you may never stop! Thousands of people stick with martial arts all their lives. As well as being fun to perform, they can help you get really fit and give you confidence.

▼ A group of young karate students in action. Learning new moves with others is lots of fun.

Throws and blows

Some people practise martial arts moves without competing against others. But many others enjoy taking part in competitions. These are mostly contests between two people with referees and judges watching and keeping score. The contestants score points for good moves such as an accurate kick or punch or a fast, controlled throw.

▼ Judo throws can be spectacular as Ilias Iliadis of Greece proves. He's on top as he throws his Japanese opponent, Hiroshi Izumi, to the floor.

▲ Three young martial artists practise a foot striking move. Their teacher looks on to correct any errors.

Judo is a really popular type of grappling martial art. This means that competitors try to gain an advantage by throwing their opponent to the floor. Then, they try to hold or pin their opponent to the floor to win points.

Tae kwon do is a striking sport. This means that it involves kicking and punching. There is no wrestling or holding in tae kwon do. In fact, points are taken off your score if you grab your opponents or throw them to the ground.

Kickboxing is a striking sport in which the speed and power of kicks and punches are important. Just as vital are defence and avoiding your opponent's attacks.

Martial arts clothing

Most martial arts are performed in bare feet. Each martial art has its own uniform. In karate, this is a thin cotton jacket and trousers called a *gi*. In tae kwon do, the outfit is similar, coloured white, and called a *dobok*. A judo outfit is called a *judogi*. It is thicker and worn looser than the karate jacket. This is because judo involves wrestling and grabbing hold of your opponent's jacket.

Most martial arts uniforms come with a belt or sash. These are coloured to indicate your rank or grade at the martial art. The photos in this book show a range of belts.

▼ A martial arts teacher will show you how to wear your clothing and tie your belt.

The highest grades

A 10th dan black belt is the highest rank possible in karate. Japan's Hirokazu Kanazawa is the only living person in the world to be one!

A black belt in judo isn't the highest possible grade. A red and white belt is awarded to someone who reaches a grade above black belt.

As you learn more and improve, you will change belts. Most of the time you will only compete against someone with the same colour belt as you.

Everyone who takes part in a martial art has to take safety very seriously. Kickboxers, for example, wrap their hands with a long roll of material like a big bandage. This helps protect them from injuries.

When fighting against someone else in kickboxing and other martial arts, you have to wear lots of safety gear, including a helmet. In tae kwon do, for example, you wear a helmet, a padded trunk protector and padded guards on your arms, your lower legs and around your groin.

▲ This kickboxer is using a handwrap to protect his hands. Handwraps are wrapped around the hand, knuckles and wrist in certain ways.

▼ This martial artist is ready for action. She wears a jacket, a belt and padded gloves and a headguard.

Schools and teachers

Martial arts are not sports you can learn at home or just with friends. You do need to go to regular classes and practice sessions. These are held at schools, sports clubs and gyms. In many martial arts, the place where you learn the martial art is called a *dojo*.

Each *dojo* has different rules and ways in which the classes are run. All, though, insist that you show respect to everyone else there, especially the martial arts teacher. He or she is often called *Sensei*.

Your martial arts teacher will take you through a warm-up. This prepares your mind and body for training. The

► These two young martial artists bow to each other before they start sparring. Bowing is a sign of respect in martial arts.

teacher will then show you new moves as well as asking you to practise and improve moves you already know.

When you practise your moves against another person this is called sparring. Sparring is a good way of improving your skills. You never have to spar against an opponent unless you want to.

▲ Many moves are practised in groups. Everyone follows the movements of the teacher.

Your teacher may give you some exercises and practices for you to do at home. But apart from these, you should never use your martial arts skills away from your classes.

▼ Each move in martial arts has to be performed perfectly. Here, a teacher adjusts one student's stance (see page 18).

Martial arts stars

A handful of top martial artists find work in movies helping with stunts. Some, such as Chuck Norris, Jean-Claude van Damme and Jackie Chan, later become major film stars.

Most martial arts champions, though, are not wealthy or famous outside their sport. They perform martial arts out of a love of

▼ Two members of Taiwan's women's judo team perform a practice bout (see page 16) in front of their coach (left).

the sport and push themselves to be as good as they possibly can. Some top champions become respected teachers and open schools to train new martial artists.

To become a martial arts champion takes a huge amount of training. Champions have to dedicate themselves to their sport. They train and practise every day and eat very healthily.

▲ Mexico's Guillermo Perez celebrates winning an Olympic gold medal for tae kwon do. He defeated Yulis Gabriel Mercedes of the Dominican Republic.

Before training, champions stretch their bodies for long periods. Stretching improves flexibility and helps them to bend their bodies in all directions. They may also prepare their minds by meditating. This relaxes them and clears their minds of thoughts other than the competition or training session ahead.

Judo

Judo means "gentle way" in Japanese. It is a wrestling-style martial art which developed out of another martial art called ju-jitsu. People who perform judo are called *judoka*.

Judoka use timing and skill rather than force to throw their opponents to the ground. In judo you use the force of your opponents' movements against them. This means that smaller *judoka* can still win fights, called bouts. It also makes judo a great martial art to learn for self-defence.

A judo bout takes place on a mat called a *tatami*. Bouts for adults are usually five minutes long for men and four minutes for women. Timings for junior bouts vary.

The scoring system in judo

The two most important types of points scored during a judo bout are *ippon* and *waza-ari*. You are awarded *ippon* if you perform a perfect throw which lands your opponent on his or her back. This wins you the bout.

You can also be awarded *ippon* if you hold your opponent on the mat for a long period or if he or she gives up by banging on the mat twice. This is called submission.

Waza-ari is really half an *ippon*. You are awarded *waza-ari* if you make a good but not perfect throw or manage to hold your opponent on the mat for a shorter time. Scoring two *waza-ari* wins you the bout.

▲ These two *judoka* are in the middle of a bout. They hold onto each other's jackets and look for a chance to strike.

▲ The female *judoka* uses her right foot to sweep her opponent's leg away. She hopes to unbalance him so that she can throw him.

In judo you can grab hold of your opponent's jacket as you wrestle for an advantage. You try to throw your opponent over your shoulder, hip or leg onto the mat. Once on the mat, you try to hold or pin your opponent on the mat to score points.

A referee walks round the mat. To interrupt a bout, the referee calls, "Matte". Then the two *judoka* must move away from each other.

▲ The referee signals that a hold on the mat has been successful. *Ippon* is scored and the *judoka* who is on top has won the bout.

Karate

Karate means "empty hand" in Japanese. It is a martial art without weapons which was designed for self-defence. Karate began on some islands off the coast of Japan. People who learn karate are called *karateka*.

There are three different parts of karate. *Kihon* is practising the basic techniques such as your stance (how you stand) and the most common kicks, punches and defensive movements. Defence includes moves called *uke*. These use parts of the hand or arm to block an opponent's punch or kick.

▶
The *karateka* on the left uses his left hand and arm to block an attack from his opponent. At the same time, he launches a strike to his opponent's body.

Kata are short patterns of movement involving punches, steps, kicks and other moves. There are over 100 *kata*. Karate students practise groups of *kata* in a row, a bit like a dance.

Kumite is the third part of karate and it involves sparring with an opponent. Karate bouts are usually short but the action is intense. In most competitions, judges award points when one *karateka* completes a good move.

▲ This *karateka* is performing a Mae Geri move. This is a front kick with the lower part of the leg snapped forward.

If one *karateka* gets eight points ahead, the bout stops and he or she is the winner.

◄

Taiwan's Chen Yen Hui aims a high kick at her opponent during the 2006 Asian Games. Karate has been part of the Asian Games since 1994.

Tae kwon do

Tae kwon do is the national sport of South Korea. *Kyorugi* is the sparring form of tae kwon do. People in more than 130 countries take part in tae kwon do. It is an Olympic sport too.

The action in tae kwon do bouts is fast and furious. You have to stay balanced and on your feet as you sway and avoid your opponent's punches and kicks.

A tae kwon do bout usually lasts three rounds. The bout takes place on a mat that is 12 metres square. Points are awarded by three judges. To score a point, you have

▶

Two young martial artists practise their tae kwon do moves. The boy in red tries to make a fist strike but is struck in the stomach with a side kick by his opponent.

to strike one of the target areas on your opponent's body with your foot or fist. The target areas are the head, the front and sides of the body.

As your legs are longer and more powerful than your arms, most of the moves that score points are kicks. These include spectacular moves such as jumping side kicks, where you fly through the air, turn your body and strike with the heel or sole of your foot.

Tae kwon do

Steven Lopez of the USA became the first person to win two Olympic gold medals in tae kwon do. He won the lightweight division at the 2000 and 2004 games.

If you pretend to be injured in a bout to get a rest, you can lose half a point from your score. This is called a *kyong-go*.

In 1956 Korean tae kwon do teacher Jhoon Rhee arrived in America with less than 50 dollars in his pocket. He would go on to teach tae kwon do to thousands of people including Bruce Lee and Muhammad Ali.

▼ Bineta Diedhiou of Senegal makes a spectacular high kick to her opponent's head. In Olympic competition, a clean strike to the head or neck with the foot is worth two points.

▼ You must wear a padded trunk protector when sparring with others. The coloured parts of the protector show the scoring areas.

Kickboxing

Kickboxing grew out of other martial arts such as karate and tae kwon do. It is a mixture of regular boxing along with kicks and blocks.

There are many forms of kickboxing including Muay Thai. This is Thailand's national sport and is very tough. Boxing gloves are the only protection that Muay Thai fighters wear. Fighters are allowed to strike with their elbows and knees as well as their hands and feet.

Other types of kickboxing are less painful. Semi-contact kickboxing only allows punches and kicks and these have to be above the waist.

▼ Champion kickboxer Anatoly Nasyrev (left) blocks a kick with his right arm whilst striking with a left-handed punch.

Kickboxers use punches that come from boxing. These include the jab which is the most common punch. Kickboxers learn ways of blocking punches and kicks. They also bob and sway out of reach of an opponent's attack.

There are many different kicking moves. The axe kick is one of the most spectacular. You lift your leg up very high and then chop it down, like an axe. Skilful kickboxers try to launch a punch and a kick one after another. This is called a combination.

Some kickboxers never spar with a real opponent. Instead, they practise their moves on pads and punchbags for exercise and for fun.

▲ You can practise your kicks and punches on a large punchbag. This kickboxer is performing a straight jab punch.

▲ Focus pads or mitts are padded blocks held by a kickboxing coach. They provide you with a moving target at which to aim your kicks and punches.

▲ Kickboxers often practise their stance and their movements in front of a full-length mirror.

▼ These two young kickboxers both attempt an attack. The boxer on the left performs a jab punch. The boxer on the right attempts a powerful roundhouse kick.

Kung fu

Kung fu is a Chinese martial art that is many centuries old. There are many different schools of kung fu.

Kung fu clothing is different from clothing worn in other martial arts. It is often black, although colours thought to be lucky in China, such as red and yellow, are also worn. Instead of being loose and tied with a belt as in judo and karate, kung fu outfits are buttoned up at the front.

Kung fu has dozens of different moves. Some are throws and holds similar to other martial arts but many others are copied from the movement of creatures in nature. These include the speedy striking of snakes and shaping your hand like a tiger's claw.

▼ These young martial artists are learning kung fu. Their teacher shows them moves and they copy him.

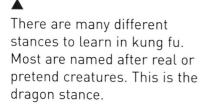

▲ There are many different stances to learn in kung fu. Most are named after real or pretend creatures. This is the dragon stance.

▲ The crane bird is said to represent patience and grace. People adopting the crane stance and moves try to keep their opponents at a distance before striking.

▲ The leopard is all about speed. People fighting leopard style aim to attack with short, sharp moves.

Tai chi is a form of kung fu. This is mostly practised as a series of slow, flowing movements. Tai chi is used as daily exercise by tens of millions of Chinese people.

► A teenager practises a kung fu move in front of the Olympic Stadium in Beijing.

Kung fu

The Epo Kung Fu School in Dengfeng, China has 6,800 students. It is one of 80 kung fu schools in and around Dengfeng.

The first ever kung fu reality TV show began in 2006. Competitors aimed to win the K-Star Chinese Kung Fu Star as they were trained by kung fu experts and watched on television.

The world of martial arts

Martial arts competitions happen all over the world. Many games such as the Asian Games and the Pan-American Games which feature a range of different of sports include some martial arts. Karate, for example, first featured in the Pan-American Games in 1995.

Two martial arts are Olympic sports. Judo first appeared in 1964. Tae kwon do was demonstrated at the 1988 Olympics and became a full sport (in which players compete for medals) in 2000.

▶
A karate bout at the 2007 Pan Arab Games which took place in Cairo, Egypt.

In most competitions the competitors are divided into different weight groups. This means that you don't have to be tall or huge to be successful at martial arts. Ryoko Tani is only 1.46m tall. Yet, she has won an amazing seven World Championships and two Olympic gold medals in judo.

Karate's biggest competition is the World Championships. These were first held in 1970. They are now held every two years, each time in a different country. The 2010 competition will be held in Belgrade, in Serbia.

Kickboxing has many different organisations which hold competitions. This can mean that there are dozens of world champions, all at the same time. Like boxers, kickboxers often fight in single bouts, rather than competing in a championship.

▼ Judo star Ryoko Tani throws Frederique Jossinet to the ground during the 2004 Olympics. Tani won a gold medal here to add to her seven World Championships.

Where next?

These websites and books will help you find out more about martial arts.

Websites

http://www.theshotokanway.com/
There is lots of information on karate at this website, including advice and tips for beginners.

http://www.wtf.org/
The home page of the World Tae kwon do Federation is a very useful site. It explains some of the basics of tae kwon do. It also lists major competitions.

www.judoinfo.com
There is plenty to read and learn at this website about judo training and moves. There are useful links to other websites too.

http://www.wkausa.com
For older readers, this website contains rules and results as well as a long list of kickboxing clubs and websites.

http://www.expertvillage.com/video-series/786_kung-fu-kids.htm
This great webpage contains 15 short videos for young people on how to perform basic kung fu moves.

http://www.karateworld.org/
This is the website for the World Karate Federation, the biggest organisation involved in karate.

www.ijf.org
A big website with a hall of fame for champions, results of competitions and tips on many of judo's most common moves.

Books

Martial Arts for Children by Nathan Johnson (Mason Crest Publishers, 2005)
This series of books provides an introduction to the history and practice of each of the martial arts.

Martial arts words

blocks moves used to stop an opponent's punch or kick from striking the intended target area

bout a contest between two people in most martial arts

combination a series of punches and kicks thrown one after another

dan a level of ability or grade in many martial arts

dobok the white outfit worn by someone practising tae kwon do

dojo the place where people learn and practise many martial arts

judoka a person who takes part in judo

karateka a person who learns and performs karate

Muay Thai also known as Thai boxing, this is kickboxing where knees, elbows and low kicks are allowed during a bout

roundhouse kick a martial arts move in which you swing your foot and leg up and around in a circle to perform a kick

Sensei the name given to many martial arts teachers or coaches

sparring training by competing as if in competition. Martial artists usually wear full protective clothing and headgear for sparring

stance the way you stand and position your body during martial arts movements

submission giving up in a martial arts bout because you are in an impossible position or in pain. Usually, a submission means you lose the contest

Index